Sports Illustrated KIDS

GREATEST MATCHES IN FOOTBALL

BY DANIEL NUNN

raintree

a Capstone company — publishers for children

Raintree is an imprint of Capstone Global Library Limited, a company incorporated in England and Wales having its registered office at 264 Banbury Road, Oxford, OX2 7DY – Registered company number: 6695582

www.raintree.co.uk
myorders@raintree.co.uk

Editorial credits
Edited by Erika L. Shores
Designed by Sofiia Rovinskaia
Media research by Jo Miller
Production by Tori Abraham

Acknowledgements
We would like to thank the following for permission to reproduce photographs: Associated Press: Hussein Malla, 27, Getty Images: Alex Livesey - UEFA, 5, Ben Radford, 11, Buda Mendes, 8, Harriet Lander, 17, Jasper Juinen, 25, Kevork Djansezian, 29, Mike Hewitt, 19, Robert Cianflone, 23, Shaun Botterill, 21, Shutterstock: FocusStocker, Cover, (top); Sports Illustrated: Neil Leifer, Cover (bottom both), 7, 13, Robert Beck, 14, SI Cover, 15. Design Elements: Shutterstock: Gojindbefs, Kucher Serhii (football), Lifestyle Graphic, Navin Penrat

978 1 3982 5861 7

British Library Cataloguing in Publication Data
A full catalogue record for this book is available from the British Library.

CONTENTS

Words in **BOLD** are in the glossary.

A MATCH TO REMEMBER?

What makes a football match one of the greatest matches of all time? It could be a star performance from one of the world's greatest players. It could be a winning goal in **stoppage time** or a **penalty shoot-out** needed to decide the winner.

A great match could be an amazing comeback, where a team has come from behind to win when no one expected it. It could be a high-scoring thriller, or perhaps a match packed with **red cards** or stunning **free kicks**. Or maybe it was a final score that no one saw coming – the kind of result that leaves fans shaking their heads in disbelief.

One thing is certain: the greatest matches in football are the matches that fans remember long after the final whistle has blown!

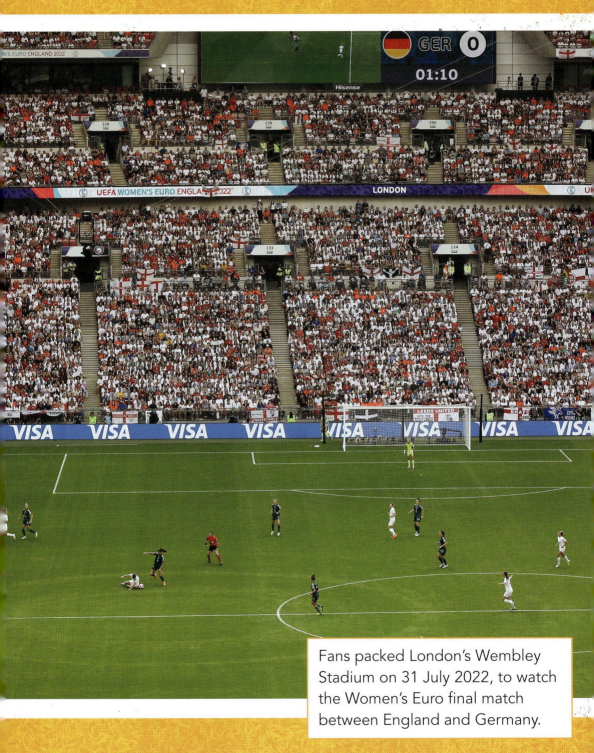

Fans packed London's Wembley Stadium on 31 July 2022, to watch the Women's Euro final match between England and Germany.

THE WORLD'S GREATEST PLAYERS

The FIFA World Cup is the most important competition in world football. Two World Cup finals, 52 years apart, starred two of the game's greatest ever players.

PELÉ INSPIRES BRAZIL

Brazilian **striker** Pelé had already won the World Cup twice. But the 1970 World Cup final made him the most famous footballer ever. The 1970 competition was the first to be beamed live around the world via satellite. It was also the first tournament to be broadcast in colour.

More than 100,000 fans filled Azteca Stadium in Mexico City to watch Brazil beat Italy 4–1 in the final. Pelé scored Brazil's first goal and provided **assists** in two of Brazil's other goals. Pelé and Brazil had won the World Cup for a record third time.

Brazilian striker Pelé (right) in action during the 1970 World Cup final

After winning the World Cup for the third time in 1970, Brazil were allowed to keep the trophy.

MESSI'S QATAR WORLD CUP TRIUMPH

Playing for Argentina and Spanish team Barcelona, Lionel Messi had won many of the game's biggest prizes. But he had never won the World Cup. At the age of 35, the 2022 World Cup in Qatar would be his last chance. Argentina made it to the final. Standing in the way was France and their superstar **striker** Kylian Mbappé.

Lionel Messi scores Argentina's third goal in the 2022 World Cup final.

The final was incredible. Argentina took a two-goal lead, including a **penalty** scored by Messi. Then France and Mbappé scored twice to take the match to **extra time**. Argentina took the lead again through a second Messi goal. However, France refused to give up. Mbappé scored a third goal to take the match to a penalty shoot-out.

Argentina went on to win the shoot-out 4–2. Messi finally had his World Cup winner's medal!

ANOTHER ARGENTINE LEGEND

In 1986, Argentina won the World Cup with the help of another superstar, Diego Maradona. Maradona was player of the tournament and scored one of the greatest goals of all time, dribbling past five players to score in a quarter-final match against England.

LATE DRAMA

Sometimes a football match is so close that, right until the end, no one can tell who will win. But then something happens late on that means that no one will ever forget it.

CHAMPIONS LEAGUE HEROICS

For 90 minutes, the 1999 Champions League final between English team Manchester United and German team Bayern Munich was nothing special. Bayern scored an early free kick, and for most of the match it looked like they would hold on to win.

But everything changed in stoppage time. First, United **substitute** Teddy Sheringham scored to level the match. Then, while Bayern were still recovering, United got a corner kick. David Beckham swung in the ball and another substitute, Ole Gunnar Solskjaer, pushed it into the net to score a stunning win for United.

Manchester United's Teddy Sheringham aims towards the goal.

A SIX-GOAL THRILLER

Although modern football was invented there, England had never won the World Cup. Then in 1966, they made it to the final where they faced West Germany. England were winning 2–1 until the 90th minute when the Germans equalized. This took the match into extra time.

England went ahead once more with a goal that is still being argued about more than 50 years later! The ball hit the underside of the crossbar and bounced right onto the goal line. The goal was given. The German players were furious. However, England went on to secure the win with another goal in the last minute. This 1966 victory remains the England men's team's only World Cup trophy so far.

England players celebrate as their third goal crosses the line. Or did it?!

WORLD CUP FINAL HAT TRICKS

A hat trick is when one player scores three goals in a single match. In the 1966 World Cup final, three of the goals were scored by England's Geoff Hurst. France's Kylian Mbappé also scored a hat trick in the 2022 final.

USA WORLD CUP GLORY

Held in the United States, the 1999 Women's World Cup attracted huge crowds and record numbers of TV viewers. Nearly 1 billion people tuned in to watch the final between the United States and China.

The Pasadena Rose Bowl stadium was packed with 90,185 fans. This made it the most attended women's sporting event of its time. However, the match itself ended 0–0, even after extra time. The winner would be decided by a penalty shoot-out.

China's third penalty was saved by US goalkeeper Briana Scurry. Both sides scored their next two penalties, meaning one more US goal would win it. Brandi Chastain stepped up to score and win the World Cup with the very last kick of the match.

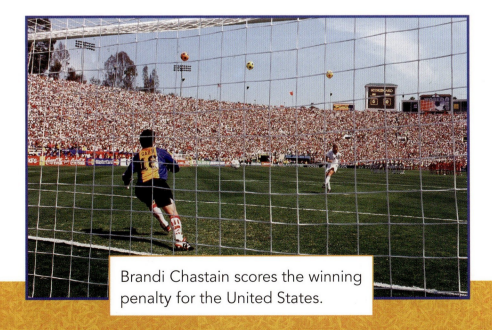

Brandi Chastain scores the winning penalty for the United States.

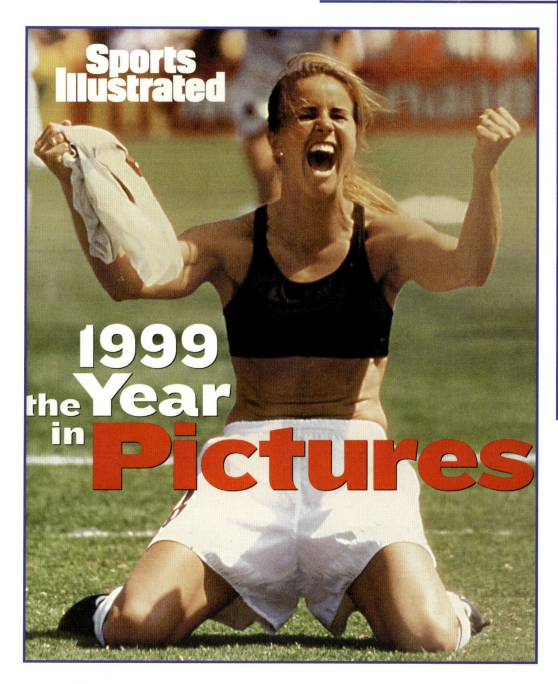

Sports Illustrated

1999
the Year
in Pictures

Sports Illustrated photographer Robert Beck's famous photograph of Brandi Chastain celebrating her goal was used on the covers of magazines such as *Sports Illustrated* and *Newsweek*.

ENGLAND BREAKS A 56-YEAR LOSING STREAK

No England team, men's or women's, had won a major tournament since 1966. But after a successful tournament at the 2022 Women's Euros, England made it to the final against Germany.

The 2022 Women's Euros boosted the popularity of women's football in Europe. Millions watched on TV, and 87,192 fans packed Wembley Stadium in London to watch the final.

After a tense 90 minutes, the match was tied 1–1. The match went to extra time and looked like it might go to penalties. Then, on 110 minutes, substitute Chloe Kelly poked the ball into the net from close range to send the England fans wild. The women's team had won England's first major trophy in 56 years.

Women were banned from playing professional football in England for more than 50 years. In 1921, the Football Association said, "The match of football is quite unsuitable for females and ought not to be encouraged."

England players celebrate with the trophy after winning the Women's Euros in 2022.

STUNNING COMEBACKS

Nothing is sweeter for a fan than watching their team come from behind to win when everyone thought they would lose.

THE MIRACLE OF ISTANBUL

The 2005 European Champions League final held in Istanbul, Turkey, was between Italy's AC Milan and England's Liverpool. The match started badly for the English side. AC Milan took the lead in the very first minute and were winning 3–0 by half-time.

The second half was a different story. Liverpool scored three goals in the space of six minutes to tie the match. The team then went on to win the penalty shoot-out 3–2 to win the trophy. One of the greatest comebacks of all time, the match became known as the "Miracle of Istanbul".

Xabi Alonso scores Liverpool's third goal to tie the match.

MANCHESTER MADNESS

Manchester United won the English Premier League 12 times between 1993 and 2011. Rivals Manchester City had not finished at the top of the league since 1968. But in 2012, all City needed to do to become champions was to win their final match of the season against Queens Park Rangers (QPR). Otherwise, United could become champions again.

City took the lead shortly before half-time. In the second half, however, City was stunned by two QPR goals. As the clock hit 90 minutes, City fans around the stadium were in tears. United fans watching at home started to celebrate.

But then, after 92 minutes, something incredible happened. First, City tied the match through an Edin Dzeko goal. Then, City's Sergio Agüero found the net again to make it 3–2 to City. City had done it, and were finally champions after a wait of 44 years.

United used to have a banner at their stadium to remind City fans of the number of years since City had last won a trophy.

Manchester City's Sergio Agüero celebrates with the Premier League trophy.

UNBELIEVABLE FINAL SCORES

Some final scores are so unbelievable that they are still remembered years later – whichever team you support.

BRAZIL HIT FOR SEVEN

As hosts of the 2014 World Cup and roared on by thousands of fans, many people thought Brazil would win the tournament. But, facing Germany in the semi-final, Brazil's World Cup dream turned into a nightmare.

Two key Brazilian players, Neymar and captain Thiago Silva, were unable to play. Then, once the match had begun, Germany raced to a five-goal lead within the first 29 minutes.

Germany added two more in the second half before Brazil finally got one back to make the final score 7–1. Brazil's World Cup was over. Germany then beat Argentina in the final. But it was this astonishing semi-final score that no one would ever forget.

The ball hits the back of the net as Thomas Müller scores Germany's first goal.

JOSE MOURINHO'S PAIN IN SPAIN

Matches between Spanish giants Barcelona and Real Madrid are one of world football's greatest events. The rivalry even has its own nickname. It's called "El Clásico" – the classic.

A 2010 Spanish La Liga match between Barcelona and Real Madrid featured some of the game's biggest superstar players and managers. Barcelona were managed by Pep Guardiola, and Madrid were led by José Mourinho.

Madrid's hopes were high! The team had just won seven league matches in a row, and their team was packed with star players, such as Cristiano Ronaldo, Sergio Ramos and Karim Benzama. Incredibly, though, Barcelona went on to win the match 5–0, with great performances from Andrés Iniesta, Xavi Hernández, Lionel Messi and David Villa.

It was the worst defeat of Mourinho's career. That year's El Clásico was definitely a classic – as long as you didn't support Real Madrid!

Real Madrid defender Pepe looks on as David Villa's shot goes past goalkeeper Casillas to make the score 3–0.

GOALS GALORE!

There is one thing that fans like to see more than anything else: goals, goals and more goals.

OLYMPIC GOAL-FEST

The US women's team had already won Olympic gold three times. At the 2012 Games, however, they nearly got a huge shock playing Canada in the semi-final.

Canada took the lead through a Christine Sinclair goal, before Megan Rapinoe scored for the United States to make it 1–1. Sinclair and Rapinoe each scored another to take the score to 2–2. Sinclair then scored a third time to complete a hat trick. It looked like Canada would be going to the final, but then the US's Abby Wambach equalized with a penalty.

After 30 minutes of extra time, the match was still a draw. But then, with almost the last kick of the match, the US's Alex Morgan headed in a last-gasp winner. The Canadians were devastated, but the match will be remembered as an all-time classic.

The United States' Megan Rapinoe (left) and Canada's Christine Sinclair scored five goals between them in this 4–3 thriller.

MLS CUP CLASSIC

The 2022 MLS Cup final between Los Angeles FC and Philadelphia Union was a match that had everything.

With the score level at 2–2 after 90 minutes, the match went into extra time. In extra time, Los Angeles FC's goalkeeper Maxime Crépeau was shown a red card and carried off on a stretcher after injuring himself fouling Philadelphia's Cory Burke.

Jack Elliott then scored for Philadelphia, before Los Angeles superstar substitute Gareth Bale equalized once more in stoppage time. Los Angeles went on to win the penalty shoot-out 3–0, with substitute goalkeeper John McCarthy (who was born in Philadelphia) saving two of Philadelphia's three penalties.

THE GREATEST MATCH OF ALL TIME?

All of the matches in this book were special. But many others could have been included too. Do you have a favourite football team? And if so, did your team make the list? If not, maybe you could compile your own list of the "Greatest Matches in Football".

Los Angeles FC's Gareth Bale levels the match at 3–3 to force penalties

GLOSSARY

assist when a player passes the ball to the scorer of
a goal

extra time time added when a football match ends in a
draw, usually in a knockout match where one side needs
to win

free kick when a team is allowed to kick the ball while
the opposing players are kept at a distance, usually after a
foul has been committed

penalty free shot on goal taken from the penalty spot,
with only the goalkeeper allowed to try to save the shot

penalty shoot-out way of deciding a match that has
ended in a draw. Both teams take penalty kicks and the
team scoring the most is the winner.

red card when a player is sent off for breaking the rules,
for example by committing a bad foul

stoppage time time added at the end of each half of
a match to make up for any time that was lost due to
injuries or substitutions; it is also sometimes called injury
time or added time

striker attacking player

substitute replacement player that is swapped for
another player on the pitch during the match

FIND OUT MORE

BOOKS

Football School Epic Heroes: 50 True Tales That Shook the World, Alex Bellos and Ben Lyttleton (Walker Books, 2020)

The Ultimate Guide to Women's Football, Emily Stead (Scholastic, 2020)

Unbelievable Football: The Most Incredible True Football Stories – The England Edition, Matt Oldfield (Wren & Rook, 2022)

WEBSITES

fifa.com
Visit the official FIFA website.

www.bbc.co.uk/bitesize/articles/z7qf6v4
Read about more great football moments from Premier League history on the BBC Bitesize website.

www.beano.com/posts/england-football-facts
Discover more fun football facts with The Beano.

INDEX

ABOUT THE AUTHOR

Daniel Nunn is the author of dozens of non-fiction books for young readers. He is a huge football fan and enjoys going to both men's and women's football matches with his children. His favourite team is Manchester City, so in his opinion, the greatest football match ever is the one on pages 20–21 of this book!